Changing Spirits
From Beer Cans To God

The poems of a recovering alcoholic

To Beverly May God Bless you always

By B.F. Simpson Jr.

11-16-97

L&B Press
San Diego, California

Changing Spirits
From Beer Cans To God
The poems of a recovering alcoholic
By B.F. Simpson Jr.

In Memory of...

Billy F. Simpson Sr.
Oct. 1928 to Sept. 1996
My Father

Dedicated to:
My wife Linda, daughters Stephenie, and Jennifer.
To the members of St. James Lutheran Church, also to my
co-workers and friends at Continental Graphics, and all the
members of A.A. for all their understanding and support.
Most of all to my parents Bill and Edith Simpson,
who loved me even when I didn't love myself.

To all of you , Thank you for being part of my life.

For additional copies of this book:

L&B Press
981 Dunning Circle
San Diego, CA 92154

Copyright © 1997 B.F. Simpson Jr. All Rights Reserved. No part of this book may be reproduced in part or in whole without the express written permission of the author. Printed in the USA.
ISBN 0-9659318-0-3

ABOUT THE BOOK

The poems contained in this book, are my emotions and feelings, put on paper for you to examine. These poems are thought provoking, and you may find a little of yourself between the lines. The words here have helped me to maintain my sobriety for over three years (at the time of publishing). When I find myself in a depressed state, I'll read some of these poems and realize how far I've come in a short time. If you find yourself in need of help, call your local office of Alcoholics Anonymous, or your operator to find the organization for your specific problem.

I am not a doctor. I'm a writer. I don't always see the good things that happen in the lives of others. If this book helps you in any way I would love to hear from you.

God Bless You,
B.F.Simpson Jr.
BSpoems@aol.com

TO THE READER

To those of you that read these poems,
keep an open mind.
Search the meaning of each phrase,
and yourself you just might find.

These poems reflect the life I lead,
the pain and sorrows felt.
I've shared these verses with you,
in hopes that they may help.

My life has changed dramatically,
since the last time I took a drink.
I no longer try to destroy myself,
or take life to the brink.

Happiness is something I've missed,
but today it's everywhere.
People seem more helpful,
they've really shown they care.

So as you read, remember,
that things in life can change.
Nothing good comes easy,
but good is within your range.

God Bless
B.F.Simpson Jr.

TABLE OF CONTENTS

7	The Hole
8	The Demon
10	The Difference
11	Only Me
12	Worries
13	The Wreckage
14	The Wall
15	Real Beauty
16	Words
17	Recovery
18	One Day At A Time
19	The Abuse
20	Heroes
22	The Riders
24	The Gift
25	The Light
26	The Example
27	The Prayer
28	The Steps
30	Kindness
31	Stress
32	The Bright New Day
34	Peace
35	My Someone
36	Fears
38	The Man In The Water
40	Passion
41	Hope
42	The Cross
44	Pain
46	Wings Of Eagles

Table of Contents (cont.)

48	The Oak
49	What Is A Friend
50	The Window To My Soul
51	Shadows Of Fear
52	A Good Man
53	My World
54	A Change
56	My Friend
57	A Choice
58	Molded By The Master
60	A Lonely Man
61	Thanking God
62	The Race
64	The World Today
66	Our Children Our Future
67	Wonders
68	The Voice
70	What's In Store
71	The Forgotten
72	Set Them Free
73	A New Day
74	You
75	The Planet
76	My Journey
78	My Little Soldier By Amy LaBruyere
79	To My Dad

THE HOLE

I've drank my share of beer and wine,
and your share too I think.
I've dug a hole of miseries,
into which I sink.

My life was filled with lies you see,
the kind that hurt me most.
Trying to be someone other than me,
but never coming close.

The person that hid within me,
is quite a sight to see.
He is a man of feelings,
he's the man I'm supposed to be.

With love and support from others,
to guide me through each day.
The man that hid inside me,
will see the light of day.

Remember the hole of miseries,
I dug so deep and wide?
A place so dark and dreary,
an easy place to hide.

Today it's very shallow,
filled by my own neglect.
Today I don't use it,
I've found my self-respect.

THE DEMON

I've tried to drink like others,
only drinking just a few.
But I always seem to lose the count,
the closer I get to two.

Then I start the journey,
to oblivion once more.
From bar to bar and club to club,
and finally my front door.

Where I was the night before,
I really couldn't say.
The only thing I'll tell you,
is that my demon knew the way.

He led me down the dark streets,
and the alleys of this town.
Through every light and stop sign,
until my house he found.

The next thing I remember,
is waking up here with you.
This place is unfamiliar,
and the people here are too.

None of them are drinking,
and there's a smile on every face.
They shake my hand in welcome,
and say it's no disgrace.

They tell me how they got here,
a journey just like mine.
That started in a barroom,
with whiskey, beer and wine.

They told me of the demon,
that led them down this road.
He took them places I had been,
and took their very souls.

But they found a way to beat him,
and The Bible says it's true.
"Where two or more are gathered,"
the Lord will be there too.

He gathers us together,
to give us strength and hope.
We talk about our journey,
and how we've learned to cope.

A friend that helps me daily,
is what I have today.
A God that gave me freedom,
just because I prayed.

I don't worry about the demon,
my children or my wife.
I have a friend named Jesus,
who leads me through my life.

He guides my wife and children,
through everything they do.
The demon will not touch them,
he has to say adieu.

THE DIFFERENCE

So many times I've wondered,
why I do the things I do?
I've searched for the reason everywhere,
but I still don't have a clue.

The man I was a year ago,
is not the same today.
The differences between us,
are as clear as night and day.

The other me was selfish,
not caring whom he hurt.
Looking for his pleasures,
and his just desserts.

Today I am so happy,
that I'm not that other man.
I now have friends who love me,
and my God to take my hand.

ONLY ME

There was a man I used to know,
he really wasn't smart.
He used to drink all night long,
and he broke a few girls hearts.

He wasn't very happy,
tho he put himself through hell.
He never made many friends,
but he really couldn't tell.

They would hang around just long enough,
to get a drink or two.
But when his money had run out,
they would disappear from view.

His wife didn't know what had happened,
to all the money she had been saving.
He had managed to spend it all,
on the booze that he was craving.

He almost lost everything,
his home, his kids, his wife.
But he found the help that he had needed,
and it has changed his life.

The changes have been dramatic,
and it's very plain to see.
The man of whom I've spoken,
is really only me.

WORRIES

So many times we find ourselves,
locked in deep despair.
We try to find some help you see,
but no one seems to care.

So we hide our pain and misery,
from other peoples eyes.
And we let it build inside us,
until we feel like part of us has died.

We worry about the little things,
that send us on a roll.
And we worry about the big things,
where we have no self control.

I've found a way to help myself,
and it seems to work just fine.
The stress is gone, and I have no fear,
and I think that it is time.

I try to find who's in control,
of the situation at the time.
If it's not me I leave it there,
and wipe it from my mind.

I leave it in the hands of God,
to deal with as He pleases.
The rest is mine to handle now,
with calm and thought and reason.

THE WRECKAGE

I left my past behind me,
not wanting to look back.
The wreckage and the ruin,
had painted my world black.

The things I've done to others,
and all the pain I've caused.
These things they dwell within me,
and sometimes give me pause.

I try to look beyond them,
to see what the future will be.
But all I saw was loneliness,
and emptiness for me.

Unless I faced the sorrow,
and the wreckage of my past.
There will not be much happiness,
at least the kind that lasts.

THE WALL

I cannot let you close to me,
the walls I've built are strong.
I've spent many years building them,
the time was hard and long.

I worked both day and night to find,
that my wall will keep you out.
You tried to give your love to me,
but my walls created doubt.

I tried to take the love you gave,
and accept it as a gift.
But these walls of mine have kept it out,
and have begun to cause a rift.

It comes between us constantly,
a barrier from my pain.
And if by chance it should fall,
who's the one to gain??

REAL BEAUTY

Beauty is all around us,
we see it every day.
The sunrise on the desert,
or the moon reflecting on the bay.

The flowers that bloom in springtime,
that fill the air with wonderful smells.
The first snow of the winter,
that blankets wherever it fell.

These are things we notice,
because they happen before our eyes.
But there is a beauty that is everlasting,
and it comes from deep inside.

We only see the outer dressings,
and try to find the flaws.
We rarely look beneath the surface,
then judge by other's laws.

God made everything around us,
and the beauty is there to find.
Forget about the thoughts of others,
and let heaven be your guide.

WORDS

Words can be our downfall,
if we let them take their toll.
They can break a lover's heart,
and cut them to their souls.

Sometimes we speak without thinking,
and our meanings get confused.
Then others think we're heartless,
difficult and rude.

It's not the words, it's the message,
and how it is received.
We try to send one meaning,
but something different is perceived.

History can show us,
the damage words have done.
With words, many battles and wars
were started, lost and won.

So next time you send a message,
make sure your meaning is clear.
Or friends can become enemies,
and your joy can turn to fear.

RECOVERY

We think that we're recovering,
if we just don't drink today.
But there is more to getting better,
than just this phrase we say.

The road to recovery is not simple,
but please don't get me wrong.
It's a journey frot with dangers,
on a trail narrow and long.

Recovery means improvement,
to grow in all you do.
To find that better life,
that God wants for you.

Recovery brings on changes,
in the things we do and say.
But changes without improvement,
can cause a man to stray.

Life is for the living,
I've often heard it said.
But life without a purpose,
can have you wind up dead.

ONE DAY AT A TIME

I spent my life in loneliness,
even in a crowd.
I sought my isolation,
in the bottles that I downed.

I drank to hide the reality,
of the man I've come to be.
To forget about my troubles,
of which I could not flee.

My past is just a memory,
of everything I've done.
My future is full of challenges,
that I've not yet won.

Today I have people that love me,
for the person that I am.
Without drinking they tell me,
I've become a better man.

Take it slow and easy,
they tell me as I go.
One day at a time will do it,
and daily you will grow.

THE ABUSE

I spend my days thinking,
about the way things used to be.
All the pain and suffering I caused,
when I was drinking and couldn't see.

My past is now behind me,
even though it haunts me still.
The things I've done confuse me,
as if I had no will.

The cheating and the lying,
to the ones that I had loved.
Alcohol had ruined my judgment,
I had taken off the gloves.

I never became physical,
but the abuse was there the same.
The scars were left emotionally,
as though I had used a cane.

But today I am so different
from the man I was back then.
The scars are almost healed,
and will never return again.

The booze is no longer with me,
the anger and hate have left too.
Today I can see clearly
and give the love that's due.

HEROES

Alcohol has ruled my life,
for many, many years.
But what I found in recent months,
has relieved me of some fears,

Alcohol no longer controls me,
like a puppet on a string.
I found a way to combat it,
and avoid it's deadly sting.

I found that when I was drinking,
I cared only for myself.
I hid the needs of others,
high upon a shelf.

I spoke of the things, that I had done,
but not a single word was true.
When found out, I lied again,
to avoid the judgment due.

Today I don't have to lie,
and be someone I'm not.
I can be the me I am,
and live the way I was taught.

Fear can make us heroes,
when used in the right way.
Or bury us in pity,
that blocks the light of day.

But fear need not be the ruler,
over this new life I lead.
I just have to turn it over,
to a power greater than me.

My God accepts my hopes and fears,
every time I pray.
He guides me with His loving hand,
so that I might not go astray.

Now fear no longer rules me,
as it has throughout the years.
And at its timely passing,
for me, there will be no tears.

THE RIDERS

The shadows fall upon the earth,
the day is growing still.
The birds have ceased their singing,
not a peep escapes their bills.

The sky is growing darker,
our time is running out.
The clouds begin to gather,
soon there will be no doubt.

The riders start appearing,
perched upon a cloud.
Their horses dressed in armor,
the hoof beats pounding loud.

The first rider was the conqueror,
his horse was white as snow.
He has come to fight injustice,
everywhere he goes.

The second horse was fiery red,
it's rider wore a look of grief.
He has come to wage a war,
and take away our peace.

Third was a horse, black as the night.
A pair of scales in the rider's hand.
He was weighing out God's justice,
and the wrongs of every man.

Finally appeared the fourth horse,
it's coat was light and pale.
And DEATH himself was the rider,
and all the people wailed.

Forgiveness was no longer,
our time on earth was through.
The Lord has sent His judgment,
the sinner's bill is due.

THE GIFT

I've spent most of my life,
in a drunken haze.
The years have passed by,
leaving me in a daze.

I've done a lot of wrongs,
and I'm sorry for them all.
I just hope that I can fix them,
before my Master's call.

I ask His help and guidance,
at the start of every day.
And in the evening I thank Him,
for His blessings as I pray.

I try to live each day,
as though it were my last.
Trying to help whom I may,
to make up for my past.

Tomorrow is the future,
and is yet to be.
Yesterday was the past,
and are the things that used to be.

Today is the present,
because it is a gift.
So make the most of it,
and please don't cause any rifts.

THE LIGHT

I have spent a lifetime trying,
to make this world just right.
To lead the people from darkness,
and guide them to the light.

But many seem to struggle,
not wanting what I've got.
They stay hidden in the darkness,
and keep the lives they've bought.

They bought them with their misery,
with pain and suffering too.
Their happiness has vanished,
among the muck and goo.

But even though their happiness,
has disappeared from sight.
There is still a chance for freedom,
if they come into the light.

My spirit is always waiting,
to accept them all back in.
But the effort must be made by them,
to let the journey begin.

I am both, man and spirit,
I helped make all, you see.
I'm known by many titles,
but today I'm called J.C.

THE EXAMPLE

I've lived my life as an example,
a bad one at most.
I drank, and smoked, and womanized,
lied and bragged and of this I would boast.

The only things that mattered,
were the pleasures I received.
It didn't matter who was hurt,
or whom I had deceived.

Then one day I realized,
the things that I had done.
I really didn't like,
the man I had become.

I wasn't very happy,
and my world was falling apart.
My wife and child left me,
I had no solace in my heart.

Years went by, I drifted,
not knowing where I was bound.
Trying to find some freedom,
from the miseries I had found.

I finally found the peace I craved,
in a God I could understand.
Now I've come full circle,
and became a better man.

THE PRAYER

I lift my voice toward heaven,
in hopes that you will hear.
The words of a broken man,
who wants you to draw near.

The prayer I have to offer,
comes from deep within.
I am opening up my heart,
and asking you to come in.

You've been away so very long,
and it has been my fault.
I'd ask you to come visit,
and at the doorway holler, "Halt!"

My house is oh so messy,
trash and dirt is everywhere.
I'm embarrassed by the things I've done,
yet I know that you do care.

Your Son has paid the price for me,
the bible tells me so.
He suffered and was crucified,
to save my mortal soul.

So God I give my life to you,
use me as you please.
And with your help and guidance,
You will get a better me.

THE STEPS

I found a way of living,
that helps to keep me sane.
It helps me to stay happy,
even through the pain.

The road of life is rugged,
with lots of ups and downs.
But today I seem to manage,
with these simple steps I found.

I accepted that I was powerless,
over things in life you see.
And life had become unmanageable,
especially for me.

I had to find somebody,
to help me through the day.
So now the God of my childhood,
is showing me the way.

I tried to be the leader,
in everything I would do.
But every time, I'd fail.
Then I got a clue.

God must be the leader,
in everything in my life.
Without Him I'd lose everything,
my home, my kids, my wife.

So today I take an inventory,
of the kind of me I am.
Listing all my shortcomings,
as many as I can.

Then I took all my defects,
and shared them with a friend.
I told my Lord about them,
in hopes that they would end.

I asked my God to take them,
and put them far away.
He said that for a short time,
some of them must stay.

They'll help me grow in wisdom,
serenity and peace.
These things are mine forever,
to hold and cherish and keep.

I made a list of people,
whom in the past I've hurt.
And tried to make amends to them,
and many times I felt like dirt.

So I continue taking tally,
of everything I do.
And when I'm wrong I say so,
to everyone that's due.

Now daily you will find me,
down on bended knee.
Looking for knowledge,
of my God's plan for me.

Now I carry on the message,
to those who need to hear.
The message of Bill W. and Dr. Bob,
that has echoed through the years.

KINDNESS

We spend so much of our lives,
buried in fear and dread.
From the time we first awaken,
until we're safe and sound in bed.

We worry about the other guy,
what he might do or say.
We worry about how we'll react,
as we journey through our day.

We rarely see the good things,
that happen as we go.
The smiles and the thank you's,
these things can help us grow.

We focus on the negative,
the anger and the hate.
Instead of the simple kindness,
of those outside our gates.

STRESS

Times have changed in many ways,
my life has lost its stress.
I've become a better man,
I have faced the challenge and passed the test.

I use to run and hide from life,
not wanting to face my fears.
The pain and sorrow I had caused,
would bring me to the brink of tears.

I would drink myself into a stupor,
at the slightest sign of stress,
Never caring who it bothered,
thinking that I knew best.

I drove away my family,
the ones that cared the most.
My friends would only come around,
for the parties I would host.

I had become very lonely,
without a friend in sight.
Then one day it happened,
the bottom was in sight.

I felt so lost and abandoned,
that I didn't know where to go.
The darkness was filling my body,
from my head down to my toes.

When all seemed lost forever,
I found a ray of light.
It helped to heal my spirit,
and gave me the power to fight.

THE BRIGHT NEW DAY

Why is life so hard for some?
Yet easy for others to live.
Why is help so hard to receive?
Yet we're always ready to give.

Why do we hate the things we do,
when we're overcome with drink?
And hurt the ones we love the most,
and take them to the brink.

We promise to try and change our lives,
to the kind that others want.
But when the pressure gets too bad,
we return to our old haunts.

We say just one to calm us down.
Then another to get us right.
Next thing we know it's closing time,
and they are turning out the lights.

The morning comes, a new day dawns,
the sun is shinning bright.
But where we are, we do not know,
and we can't remember last night.

We realize we need some help,
but know not where to turn.
So some of us give up the fight,
and never really learn.

The rest of us will find that door.
In which we can be safe.
Where a spirit of hope and happiness,
you can see on every face.

A place where we can find a way,
to change our ways of life.
To make us more acceptable,
in other people's eyes.

Self respect is something new to us,
we found it here you see.
With people who were hopeless too,
just like you and me.

We found a God we understood,
and he helps us through our days.
He guides our steps in sobriety,
to a bright new day.

PEACE

I sit near the ocean,
watching the tidal flow.
I admire the nearing sunset,
as I feel all tension go.

I feel at peace with the world,
as the evening sky changes to a deep pink.
The stress of the day is over,
as into a dream state I sink.

My mind begins to wander,
to when times were not so hard.
When children could play freely,
without the fear of harm.

I think of all the places,
that I've visited in my past.
I remember wonderful memories,
but the years have slipped by fast.

If we could only recapture,
the values we had back then.
Life would be worth living,
instead of giving in.

MY SOMEONE

I found someone who understands,
the things I do and say.
Who shows me what is right and wrong,
to keep me from going astray.

This someone gives me feelings,
that hurt from time to time.
And lifts me when I've fallen,
into the muck and grime.

My life has been a disaster,
a hell I made myself.
But this someone takes my errors,
and puts them on a shelf.

This someone shares my journey,
through this life that we have planned.
And helps to keep me grounded,
yet not buried in the sand.

God is this special someone,
who walks with me today.
And with His help and guidance,
I won't ever go astray.

FEARS

Alcohol has ruled my life,
for oh so many years.
But what I found in recent months,
has relieved me of some fears.

Alcohol no longer controls me,
like a puppet on a string.
I found a way to combat it,
and avoid it's deadly sting.

I found that when I was drinking,
I cared only for myself.
I hid the needs of others,
high upon a shelf.

I spoke of things that I had done,
but not a single word was true.
When found out, I'd lie again,
to avoid the judgment due.

Today I don't have to lie,
and be someone I'm not.
I can be the me I am,
and live as I was taught.

Fear can make us heroes,
when used in the right way,
or bury us in pity,
that can block the light of day.

But fear need not be the ruler,
over this new life I lead.
I just have to turn it over,
to a power greater than me.

My God accepts my hopes and fears,
every time I pray.
He guides me with his loving hand,
that I might not go astray.

Now fear no longer rules me,
as it has throughout the years.
And at it's timely passing,
for me, there will be no tears.

THE MAN IN THE WATER

I was walking by a river,
in a land that I've never been.
There was a man standing in the water,
and he asked me to come in.

As I stepped into the wetness,
his robe began to glow.
I began to feel uneasy,
my fear began to grow.

He said do not be frightened,
we have a ways to go.
Touch my hand and follow me,
and I will lead you home.

We traveled to a city,
in the twinkling of an eye.
It's beauty was overcoming,
I thought I would surely die.

The walls were made of crystal,
at least that's what I thought.
But the man said they were diamonds,
from the bottom to the top.

The gates were purest silver,
and as tall as you could see.
They sparkled in the daylight,
with a certain majesty.

The man said we must hurry,
we have alot to see.
Our time is growing shorter,
so stay right next to me.

We went into the city,
and what did I behold?
Streets that stretched for miles,
made of precious gold.

We came upon a temple,
surrounded by a crowd.
Then the people started singing,
it started to get loud.

Just then a voice spoke to me,
and I jumped with quite a start.
It said I must return now,
so that I might do my part.

Remember what you've seen here,
and all the things I've done.
Your journey has only started,
you've only just begun.

Your past has been forgiven,
forgotten and wiped clean.
Tomorrow is tomorrow,
you can leave that up to me.

You only have today to live,
and do the things you can.
To love your wife and family,
and your fellow man.

Just then I did awaken,
and there above my bunk.
Was a poster that simply read,
"God does not make junk."

PASSION

As I lay here thinking of my life,
I wonder where I went wrong.
I spent so much time worrying,
with hours that were so hard and long.

I find that I was living,
without a purpose in my life.
I neglected the important things around me,
to include my children and my wife.

The passions I had were misguided,
Their directions led me astray.
I found I was going places,
but had no place to stay.

I used the passions of my mind,
to get me where I'm at.
But if I would have used my heart,
my world would not be so black.

The passions of the heart,
give us love and integrity.
But those that come from our head,
only give us insecurity.

HOPE

I've lived a life of hopelessness,
depression and despair,
My drinking left me empty,
with times of happiness that were rare.

I followed my own thinking,
to get me through the pain.
The trouble that would follow,
would take all that I had gained.

Today I have a leader,
to show me where I'm wrong.
He never passes judgment,
and forgives me all day long.

To him I am a treasure,
more precious than the gold.
He leads me as a child,
with hands so strong and bold.

My Jesus is my leader,
He teaches me to cope.
Today I am a child of God,
with love and friends and hope.

THE CROSS

I stood beside a woman,
whose face was full of tears.
As the procession passed before us,
my heart was full of fear.

A man that had been beaten,
struggled with his heavy load.
As they march him through the streets,
the insults from the crowd arose.

The burden that he carried,
was his alone to bear.
Not one of us could replace him,
nor would we even dare.

The journey to the hilltop,
was slow and long you see.
And anger filled the air,
with shouts to set this person free.

Once upon the hilltop,
the soldiers did their job.
They drove spikes through his hands and feet,
while keeping back the mob.

They slowly lifted up the cross,
and it settled with a thump.
The man was nailed to it,
and in my throat there grew a lump.

The man spoke so quietly,
and spoke for me and you.
He said, "Father forgive them,
for they know not what they do".

His final words I remember,
they seem so cool and calm.
"Father into your hands I give my spirit,
it is finished", it was done.

This man that died upon the cross,
did so for you and me.
To pay for our forgiveness,
and those of humanity.

PAIN

For as long as I can remember,
there has been pain in my life.
Most of which I caused myself,
with my rebellion and my strife.

I fought against my parents,
at every turn I made.
I fought against the teachers,
so after school I stayed.

When I started drinking,
at an innocent age of ten.
The pain began to subside,
until I sobered up again.

The bottle was my courage,
and an easy place to hide.
An escape from all those feelings,
that often made me cry.

The pain had not vanished,
it hid here deep inside.
Buried with emotions,
the ones I had to hide.

Love was hidden from me,
along with honesty and peace.
The pain was going deeper,
and my coldness would not cease.

I started using people,
to get the things of life.
I ruined every relationship,
to include those with my kids and wife.

My life was full of selfish thoughts,
not caring who was hurt.
My morals had disappeared,
and turned to dust and dirt.

Today my life has begun to change,
my feelings I now let show.
When pain begins to overwhelm,
I just let God, and let go.

WINGS OF EAGLES

I've traveled all around this world,
and I've seen many beautiful sights.
But the one I found most wondrous,
was to see a Bald Eagle in flight.

He cuts the air with majesty,
then climbs high into the sky.
With grace and ease he floats there,
how I wish that it were I.

To fly above my troubles,
would be such a great relief.
But today I have to face them,
for I've caused a lot of grief.

His strength is so apparent,
as he glides across the sky.
His life seems so peaceful,
unlike you and I.

The human race is greedy,
not caring whom they harm.
If you try to lend a hand,
they'll try to take your arm.

My drinking took my family,
and moved them far away.
With bitterness and anger,
they had become my prey.

The eagle only captures,
the things he really needs.
Never wasting what he's got,
and what he gets is free.

If we were more like eagles,
this world would seem so bright.
We would all have what we needed,
with no reason left to fight.

THE OAK

The valley lies before me,
an oak tree in its midst.
The emblem of strength and beauty,
and from where I sit it fits.

A tree so straight and majestic
that I find myself in awe,
Because my life is like a sapling,
that folds and bends and yaws.

Then Jesus came and staked me,
to give me more support.
Now as I grow in the Spirit,
the Lord is my escort.

He teaches me of wisdom,
and of the beauty in all I see.
And someday in His kingdom,
I'll be as that oak tree.

WHAT IS A FRIEND

A friend is someone that will stand by you,
through the good times and the bad.
A friend will be supportive,
when your happy, or when your sad.

A friend will not deceive you,
or try to steal you blind.
A friend, you can count on,
even in the worst of times.

A friend will give you comfort,
when you're sick and feeling down.
A friend will lift your spirits,
because a friendship has no bounds.

So be a friend to someone,
and show you really care.
Because one day you may need a friend,
and you'll want somebody there.

THE WINDOW TO MY SOUL

Words can tell a lot about you,
the way you communicate your thoughts.
Some of us speak loudly,
much louder than we ought.

Some are very quiet,
hardly saying a word.
Making people wonder,
if we might be disturbed.

For me, I write in poems,
the things I feel inside.
Like a window to my soul,
where nothing there can hide.

I find that I'm more open,
when I put my words to pen.
I can tell you what I'm feeling,
from the beginning to the end.

I try to keep it simple,
so all may understand.
My poems are only windows,
to the soul of this simple man.

SHADOWS OF FEAR

I find that all around me,
are shadows of my past.
They sometimes seem to engulf me,
in the darkness that they cast.

I find that there is pain,
in the shadows of long ago.
But if I try to dwell there,
the fear will start to grow.

I have to live today,
and put my past to rest.
Sometimes it isn't easy,
but I know it's for the best.

Because if I allow the past,
to rule me as I go.
The shadows and the fears,
could steal my very soul.

The shadows are still present,
and remind me where I was.
That's what keeps me sober,
along with lots of love.

A GOOD MAN

How can I be the man that I am?
Who is to tell me what to do?
Why do people forget each other?
What should a good man do?

I try to live one day at a time,
and show others a warm smile.
But many times you step into a hole,
that seems to go down for miles.

So many times we find ourselves,
caught in the troubles of our day.
With so much going on around us,
it's hard to see through the haze.

The small emergencies are a constant drain,
but we handle them just fine.
Then when a major catastrophe hits,
it's enough to blow our minds.

But the good man seems to manage,
and life continues on.
He always sees the good things,
and with hope and prayer, carries on.

Life is but a moment,
and you should live it to it's max.
Lest the darkness of the day consumes you,
and you find this morning was your last.

MY WORLD

I share this world with you,
and sometimes you make it hard.
We don't always see eye to eye,
but being here is a start.

We are different as night and day,
but it's that difference for which we live.
For without the difference life would be boring,
and we would have nothing left to give.

This life we live has ups and downs,
like a road full of hills.
But because we travel it together,
it has become quite a thrill.

Our paths have crossed many times,
and will again I hope.
Because without you in my world,
I find it hard to cope.

So Lord, be with me always,
and never let me stray.
For this life is worth the living,
and in your love, I'll stay.

A CHANGE

I've tried to change the world,
to make things go my way.
But every time I start,
my world goes astray.

People don't want to change,
to the way I think they should.
And I just can't understand it,
don't they know its for their own good.

I've tried to make them listen,
and show them how to act.
But they seem to just ignore me,
can you imagine that.

Don't they know who I am,
and how important I can be?
I am the leader of the race,
at least I am to me.

But today I have a new life,
that's free of pain and strife.
I only want to be an example,
to my children and my wife.

My life is no longer ruled,
by the booze I drank back then.
I've discovered that I'm human,
and there is a battle yet to win.

My war is not with humans,
no bombs or tanks or guns.
The battle is deep within me,
and it's only just begun.

To repair all the damage,
that my alcoholic mind has wrought.
To turn from hate and anger,
and love the life I've got.

So no longer am I a ruler,
or a god in my own mind.
The world will have to settle,
for me as part of humankind.

MY FRIEND

I find that I'm not alone,
in this life that I live.
So many others like me,
have so much to give.

For so much of my life,
I felt alone, not knowing what to do.
Then I found a real friend,
and I bet you're wondering who?

My friend has endured suffering,
pain and ridicule.
He didn't have a lot of friends,
but the ones he had were true.

He never seemed to judge,
the people that he met.
He was always accepting,
and had no big regrets.

My friend always had compassion,
for the people in despair.
He seems to love everyone,
no matter what they would wear.

In the end it was that love,
that set mankind free.
The carpenters son from Nazareth,
is my greatest friend indeed.

A CHOICE

So many times we seem scared,
of the troubles in this life.
We hide from the unpleasant,
and try to, forgo a fight.

We seldom stand up for what we believe in,
and let others take control.
We like to hide our feelings,
until disaster takes it's toll.

We always have an opinion,
which we hardly ever voice.
Without saying what you feel,
you give up your right of choice.

So try to make your desires known,
and speak of how you felt.
You'll find that you feel better,
with the hand of cards you're dealt.

MOLDED BY THE MASTER

As I look out over the ocean,
as the sun sinks into the sea.
I ponder all I have accomplished,
and find that God has a plan for me.

He has let me burn with anger,
in the furnace of my rage.
He has let me feel the sorrow,
as a creature in a cage.

My life was on the Masters anvil,
as He bent and formed and shaped.
My world was full of heartache,
and I tried many times to escape.

I tried to hide in a bottle,
but it only made things worse.
I'd sober up in the morning,
and with no change, I'd curse.

I blamed Him for my miseries,
and all the pain I felt.
But when I came back to reality,
I had played the hand I was dealt.

I gambled on a better day,
as soon as I sobered up.
Where everybody liked me,
but I found it a bitter cup.

As long as I was buying,
friends were all around.
But when I ran out of money,
they were nowhere to be found.

So as God's hammer strikes the metal,
and He forms me as He wills.
I become a new creature,
and my life is now a thrill.

For with God I can do anything,
I found out the hard way.
My growth will still continue,
because with Him I'll stay.

A LONELY MAN

Where am I going?
Why am I here?
What's in my future?
Will you still be there?

These are things I wonder,
as I go about my life.
I'll never find the answer,
if my world is full of strife.

I want to be accepted,
for the me I think I am.
But the world just ignores me,
for I am a simple man.

I'm not very outgoing,
and my life is really plain.
I have few friends that matter,
and sometimes they give me pain.

I want to feel the freedom,
that comes from being yourself.
But I'm afraid to let my feelings show,
so I keep them on a shelf.

One day I'll find the strength I need,
to guide me from my cave.
But until then I'll hide here,
and try to still be brave.

THANKING GOD

As I sit by the campfire,
I think of all I've done.
The battles that I've fought,
and the battles I have won.

The people that have been there,
when I needed advice; a bit.
The friends that seemed to push me,
instead of letting me quit.

I'm glad that you are with me,
even when your not in sight.
I know that you will help me,
no matter what my plight.

Through it all, God, you have been there,
only a prayer away.
The true friend, I have needed,
and a true friend you'll stay.

So as the fire slowly dies,
and the darkness creeps in.
I'll slip into slumber,
thanking you again.

THE RACE

I ask myself the question,
why am I the way I am.
In many ways I'm similar,
to every other man.

What makes me different,
and should I try to change?
These are the things I ponder,
and they cover quite a range.

My life was once in turmoil,
there was no direction for my soul.
I seem to go in circles,
always shifting with the flow.

My drinking was my downfall,
it ran my entire life.
It caused me to lose a family,
a child and a wife.

The Army didn't like it,
when I came to work still drunk.
At the time I didn't understand,
why my military career was sunk.

After thirty years of drinking,
I finally found my place.
I, like many others,
have ran the same old race.

The finish line is still ahead,
the race is not yet won.
But as long as I am sober,
I still get to run.

To lose would be disaster,
I would lose all that I have gained.
My world would turn to ruin,
and I'd never be the same.

But today, I keep on running,
with the finish line in sight.
As long as I stay sober,
my future will be bright.

THE WORLD TODAY

The world is in turmoil,
and nobody knows just why.
A bitter tone of anger strikes,
as we watch a child die.

The kids are killing each other,
because they don't look the same.
To them the facts of life and death,
are only but a game.

We need to try to teach them,
that life can be much more.
They're living without a purpose.
They seem to have closed the door.

Life is to be respected,
everyone has that right.
But the children don't understand,
so all they do is fight.

We need to be more involved,
in the things they do and say.
Show them by example,
and maybe they won't stray.

The future is in our hands,
as our children start to grow.
Without truth and understanding,
where will this world go.

So teach the ways of freedom,
that we were taught so long ago.
That morals and forgiveness,
are the better way to grow.

"Do unto others,
as you would have them do to you."
These simple words of wisdom,
today they still ring true.

OUR CHILDREN, OUR FUTURE

I look around this world,
full of violence and strife.
A lack of good judgment,
that affects every life.

With wars, criminals and disasters,
and we just turn our heads.
We feel that it won't happen to us,
but the day it does we dread.

We need to take the upper hand,
and change our point of view.
For the chance for a peaceful future,
has to begin with you.

We must set the example for our children,
and teach them right from wrong.
Or this world of ours won't be here,
and at this rate it won't take long.

Let your goodness shine around you,
and let friendship be your stand.
For the children need our guidance,
and that's the job of every man.

WONDERS

So many times we never see,
the wonders all around.
The colors of the evening sky,
as the sun is going down.

The majesty of the mountains,
as they stand before our view.
The ocean waves as they roll to shore,
that help to keep us cool.

We spend a lifetime,
caught up in our own lives.
That the wonders of our world,
are neglected in our minds.

Try to take a moment,
in your busy day.
To think about the world,
and it's wonders of today.

THE VOICE

I heard a voice calling,
it was soft and low.
Asking me to follow,
wherever it may go.

It led me into the darkness,
a place I'd never been.
It told me of a battle,
of which I could not win.

My world started changing,
with lies and hate and strife.
To the point of pure disaster,
when I almost took my life.

I felt I was lost in the darkness,
with no light to show the way.
I was only just existing,
to what extent was hard to say.

Then one day it happened,
my world was falling apart.
I had nothing left to hope for,
I felt abandoned in the dark.

I heard a new voice calling,
unlike the voice before.
This one was full of compassion,
and it lead me to a door.

It said that it had been waiting,
for me to make a choice.
Either follow him to sunlight,
or stay in the darkness with the other voice.

I had tried the darkness,
and found it was not for me.
So as the door slowly opened,
a light I began to see.

Now my life is different,
no longer full of fear.
The voice I follow is loving,
it's God's and He's always near.

WHATS IN STORE?

Where will we be ten years from now?
What does our future hold?
Will there be wars around the world?
Will we find a cure for the cold?

These questions haunt our thinking,
and we ponder these in our minds.
But tomorrow is uncertain,
and the past we leave behind.

Our children are our future,
and right now it isn't good.
Too many are turning from us,
to join gangs in the hood.

We need to remember our yesterdays,
how our lives have been back then.
Bring back the moral standards,
or our future could be our end.

Teach them that love isn't physical,
that it is the spirit of being true.
It's an emotional state of mind,
that can help us make it through.

We need to get along,
and help each other achieve.
Because if we don't, our future,
will only make us grieve.

So let's learn to forgive, and then move on.
Don't let hatred take control.
The future is in our hands;
let's make it a place of peaceful souls.

THE FORGOTTEN

There is a star shining,
far above the earth.
It's light is glowing brighter,
as the sky perceives it's birth.

We seem to over look it,
as we do many things in this life.
But we always seem to focus,
on the hatred and the strife.

The wonders all around us,
seem to disappear from view.
The sunrise on a desert,
with all it's colorful hues.

A pine tree in a forest,
with all it's beauty and strength.
Always goes unnoticed,
until it's gone without a trace.

Our lives have become too busy,
we haven't the time to care.
We worry that the other guy,
will take our rightful share.

As for me I'll sit in silence,
and watch the mysteries go by.
Then tell you of all the wonders,
that I notice before, your eyes.

SET THEM FREE

As we move into the future,
our imaginations soar.
We can make a difference,
but we know not what's in store.

A new century approaches,
with advancements good and bad.
But the future is ours to mold,
and it should be better than the past we had.

We must strive to make improvements,
in everything we do.
Because without them we will suffer,
our past has shown this true.

We control our outcome,
whether bad or good.
We can make the changes,
and I really think we should.

Education will be the foundation,
for building things anew.
Our children are our future,
help them stay in school.

They will walk on other planets,
they will cure the common cold.
They will do the things we've dreamed of,
since the days of old.

So be the kind of person,
you want your children to be.
Help them set their sights on the future,
and help set their imaginations free.

A NEW DAY

I look at the sunrise with a sense of awe;
I made it through another night.
It reminds me how dark my past was,
but today my future seems bright.

I have done many things,
that I regret in days gone by.
As I reflect back on them,
all I can do is sigh.

For all the wrongs I did back then,
I have tried to make amends.
For that was in my old life,
and today a new life begins.

Like the sky fills with color,
as the sun begins to rise.
My darkness begins to vanish,
and for me, that is a surprise.

But now I'm someone different,
like the day I am brand new.
I owe my change to God,
and all my friends like you.

YOU

I gaze into the garden,
as the daylight breaks anew.
I look upon the roses,
and can only think of you.

The beauty of this world,
pales in your sight.
For you are the one,
that can make my life seem right.

You are there when I am lonely,
you lead me by the hand.
You're there in my darkest battles,
you help me make a stand.

You loved me when I was hopeless,
and showed you really cared.
You were there to give me comfort,
whenever I was scared.

I owe you everything,
that I am today.
I would not be here,
if you had gone away.

So stay with me forever,
be my guiding light.
You are the one I count on,
Lord don't ever leave my sight.

Inspired by my friend
Laurie Draine

THE PLANET

I feel the breeze softly blowing,
as the trees around me sway.
I smell the sweet scent of the flowers,
as I start a brand new day.

I can hear the surf crashing,
as it rushes to the shore.
I can see the mountains in the distance,
as I close my front door.

These are the wonders of our world,
they are our legacy.
Without them we wouldn't be here,
mankind just wouldn't be.

The beauty of this world,
is ours to keep intact.
Let us protect it for our future,
and not destroy it with senseless acts.

We are the guardians of our planet,
we are the teachers of our kids.
We must protect this world we live on,
or none of us will live.

MY JOURNEY

I've traveled the road of life,
in a drunken foggy haze.
My world has been in turmoil,
since my younger days.

Rebellious as a child,
I rejected what was right.
My parents had their hands full,
and I was quite a sight.

I tried to fight the system,
with little or no success.
Alcohol took over,
and gave me little rest.

The more I drank, the worse I got,
but there was no turning back.
I lived to drink, I was obsessed,
my world was turning black.

For thirty years I struggled,
trying to find a way.
To end the demons torture,
and live a sober day.

I changed the way I did things,
switching from whiskey to wine.
But the only signs of slowing,
was only in my mind.

From wine to beer, bottle to can,
I tried it all you see.
People called me hopeless,
but I said, "I couldn't be."

I looked for other options,
but nothing seemed to work.
The bars no longer helped me,
or the gutter where I lurked.

I finally found the bottom,
to the hole that I had dug.
I had lost everything,
including those I loved.

I made their lives unbearable,
with all the things I had done.
I had become a shell of a man,
thank God I had no gun.

I might have tried to end it all,
but could not, even then.
I had become a coward,
unto the bitter end.

Just then a light appeared,
from where I did not know.
I followed as it drew me,
to a door that was all aglow.

Since that day I haven't drank.
They taught me what to do.
To the men and women of A.A.,
my hat goes off to you.

In Memory Of
Steven LaBruyere

Feb, 1996 to July, 1996
A little light that shined into many lives.
These words are from mother to son.

MY LITTLE SOLDIER

My little soldier of strength,
enduring all that Hell has thrown your way.
I can't imagine how such a little one,
has such a will to stay.
In a world where those supposed to be older and wiser,
choose the easier road of the coward.
The youth an innocence of a child,
stands his ground with all his power.
What a testament you are,
to the working of God's holy plan.
That through it all you put your trust,
within His mighty hand.
To uplift you in a way,
that no human ever could.
The Holy Spirit moves within,
as in all of us He should.
What an irony of life has spun,
when the example,
is such a little one.

Amy LaBruyere
Steven's mother.

TO MY DAD

You were nervous that night long ago,
you didn't get much sleep.
You paced the floor wondering,
who it was that you would meet.

Your life was full of uncertainty,
with a war going on.
But you stayed waiting,
until the early dawn.

You'll never know what you meant to me,
in those early days of life.
You were the man I looked up to,
whenever there was strife.

I hardly ever showed it,
the love I had for you inside.
Now it's too late to let it out,
it's been almost a year since you died.

But **Dad**, you're still with me,
in everything I do.
I just want to let you know,
that because of you I grew.

Your Son
Billy F. Simpson Jr.